A DAY WITH A DOG NAMED DRAGON

TRACEY FUDGE SCHEDLER

ILLUSTRATED BY AMY OLIVER

Copyright 2016 by Tracey Fudge Schedler
Illustrated by Amy Oliver
Edited by Jennifer Bogart Jaquith
Cover & Interior Layout by Joanne Kasunic

This book is a work of fiction. Names, characters, places and incidents are products of the author's imagination or are used fictitiously. Any resemblance to actual events or locales or persons, living or dead, is entirely coincidental. No dogs, birds, or plantlife were harmed in the writing of this book.

ISBN 978-0-9950569-0-9

DEDICATION

For my family, especially my children who inspire me every day with their smiles, laughter, sadness, and spunk.

ACKNOWLEDGEMENTS

Thanks to my friends at Morning Rain Publishing for guidance, support, and encouragement.

One beautiful and sunny day, Dragon, a lively and bouncy dog, ran, rolled, and frolicked in a large backyard.

Dragon was a young dog
with silver and grey shaggy fur.
He looked like someone
had dipped paintbrushes into
silver paint and then flicked
paint all over him. The only other
bits of colour on him were some
small patches of reddish fur
around his ears.

Dragon was excited for summer as it had been a long, cold, and blustery winter. Too much snow meant not enough playtime outside. He had missed playing in between the tall trees, lush green bushes, and colourful flowers.

Spring and summer were magical times, as the flowers popped up and stretched into the sky before withering away.

Spring and summer were Dragon's favourite seasons. There was always something to explore. There was always something dazzling to look at.

It was early morning, and the sun was just peeking up above the trees and shining through the branches and leaves to create brilliant colours. Vibrant shadows danced across the yard.

Dragon looked around the yard. After stalking through some gardens, he shook off some leaves and purple pansies. He rolled a few times and landed in a flower bed with dazzling daffodils, red roses, amazing azaleas, blue bells, and fiery foliage.

He blended in well due to his grey, silver, and red.

Dragon was so happy about all the wonderful colours he could see; they reminded him of a rainbow following a summer rain. It was like he had his own rainbow in his yard to look at whenever he wanted.

With the sun high in the sky,
Dragon knew it was mid-day.
He was so happy to still have
his afternoon to play and enjoy
nature.

As he contemplated what to explore next, a movement and flash of colour caught his eye. He looked up into the tall, royal-purple smokebush. The delicate leaves danced from a slight breeze, and dancing sunbeams showed off the purple and scarlet red colours.

As the afternoon went on, Dragon ran through lush bushes. He rested under cover to watch birds take a bath and to watch birds dart in and out of hidden nests in trees.

Slowly, the sun began to sink behind the tree tops and billowy clouds. Dragon sauntered over to a tree with long, low-hanging branches.

He felt really tired from his day of play and thought this would make a great place for a nap. After all, playing all day is hard work.

Tomorrow would be here soon enough, and he would get to do it all over again. He curled up and fell asleep to swaying branches and smells of nature.

The End.

72619069R00022

Made in the USA
Columbia, SC
22 June 2017